Concerning Christian Liberty

MARTIN LUTHER

Contents

Letter of Martin Luther to Pope Leo X

Among those monstrous evils of this age with which I have now for three years been waging war, I am sometimes compelled to look to you and to call you to mind, most blessed father Leo. In truth, since you alone are everywhere considered as being the cause of my engaging in war, I cannot at any time fail to remember you; and although I have been compelled by the causeless raging of your impious flatterers against me to appeal from your seat to a future council—fearless of the futile decrees of your predecessors Pius and Julius, who in their foolish tyranny prohibited such an action—yet I have never been so alienated in feeling from your Blessedness as not to have sought with all my might, in diligent prayer and crying to God, all the best gifts for you and for your see. But those who have hitherto endeavored to terrify me with the majesty of your name and authority, I have begun quite to despise and triumph over.

One thing I see remaining which I cannot despise, and this has been the reason of my writing anew to your Blessedness: namely, that I find that blame is cast on me, and that it is imputed to me as a great offence, that in my rashness I am judged to have spared not even your person.

Now, to confess the truth openly, I am conscious that, whenever I have had to mention your person, I have said nothing of you but what was honorable and good. If I had done otherwise, I could by no means have approved my own conduct, but should have supported with all my power the judgment of those men concerning me, nor would anything have pleased me better, than to recant such rashness and impiety. I have called you Daniel in Babylon; and every reader thoroughly knows with what distinguished zeal I defended your conspicuous innocence against Silvester, who tried to stain it.

Indeed, the published opinion of so many great men and the repute of your blameless life are too widely famed and too much reverenced throughout the world to be assailable by any man, of however great name, or by any arts. I am not so foolish as to attack one whom everybody praises; nay, it has been and always will be my desire not to attack even those whom public repute disgraces. I am not delighted at the faults of any man, since I am very conscious myself of the great beam in my own eye, nor can I be the first to cast a stone at the adulteress.

I have indeed inveighed sharply against impious doctrines, and I have not been slack to censure my adversaries on account, not of their bad morals, but of their impiety. And for this I am so far from being sorry that I have brought my mind to despise the judgments of men and to persevere in this vehement zeal, according to the example of Christ, who, in His zeal, calls His adversaries a generation of vipers, blind, hypocrites, and children of the devil. Paul, too, charges the sorcerer with being a child of the devil, full of all subtlety and all malice; and defames certain persons as evil workers, dogs, and deceivers. In the opinion of those delicate-eared persons, nothing could be more bitter or intemperate than Paul's language.

What can be more bitter than the words of the prophets? The ears of our generation have been made so delicate by the senseless multitude of flatterers that, as soon as we perceive that anything of ours is not approved of, we cry out that we are being bitterly assailed; and when we can repel the truth by no other pretense, we escape by attributing bitterness, impatience, intemperance, to our adversaries. What would be the use of salt if it were not pungent, or of the edge of the sword if it did not slay? Accursed is the man who does the work of the Lord deceitfully.

Wherefore, most excellent Leo, I beseech you to accept my vindication, made in this letter, and to persuade yourself that I have never thought any evil concerning your person; further, that I am one who desires that eternal blessing may fall to your lot, and that I have no dispute with any man concerning morals, but only concerning the word of truth. In all other things I will yield to any one, but I neither can nor will forsake and deny the word. He who thinks otherwise of me, or has taken in my words in another sense, does not think rightly, and has not taken in the truth.

Your see, however, which is called the Court of Rome, and which neither you nor any man can deny to be more corrupt than any Babylon or Sodom, and quite, as I believe, of a lost, desperate, and hopeless impiety, this I have verily abominated, and have felt indignant that the people of Christ should be cheated under your name and the pretext of the Church of Rome; and so I have resisted, and will resist, as long as the spirit of faith shall live in me. Not that I am striving after impossibilities, or hoping that by my labors alone, against the furious opposition of so many flatterers, any good can be done in that most disordered Babylon; but that I feel myself a debtor to my brethren, and am bound to take thought for them, that fewer of them may be ruined, or that their ruin may be less complete, by the plagues of Rome.

For many years now, nothing else has overflowed from Rome into the world—as you are not ignorant—than the laying waste of goods, of bodies, and of souls, and the worst examples of all the worst things. These things are clearer than the light to all men; and the Church of Rome, formerly the most holy of all Churches, has become the most lawless den of thieves, the most shameless of all brothels, the very kingdom of sin, death, and hell; so that not even antichrist, if he were to come, could devise any addition to its wickedness.

Meanwhile you, Leo, are sitting like a lamb in the midst of wolves, like Daniel in the midst of lions, and, with Ezekiel, you dwell among scorpions. What opposition can you alone make to these monstrous evils? Take to yourself three or four of the most learned and best of the cardinals. What are these among so many?

You would all perish by poison before you could undertake to decide on a remedy. It is all over with the Court of Rome; the wrath of God has come upon her to the uttermost. She hates councils; she dreads to be reformed; she cannot restrain the madness of her impiety; she fills up the sentence passed on her mother, of whom it is said, "We would have healed Babylon, but she is not healed; let us forsake her." It had been your duty and that of your cardinals to apply a remedy to these evils, but this gout laughs at the physician's hand, and the chariot does not obey the reins. Under the influence of these feelings, I have always grieved that you, most excellent Leo, who were worthy of a better age, have been made pontiff in this. For the Roman

Court is not worthy of you and those like you, but of Satan himself, who in truth is more the ruler in that Babylon than you are.

Oh, would that, having laid aside that glory which your most abandoned enemies declare to be yours, you were living rather in the office of a private priest or on your paternal inheritance! In that glory none are worthy to glory, except the race of Iscariot, the children of perdition. For what happens in your court, Leo, except that, the more wicked and execrable any man is, the more prosperously he can use your name and authority for the ruin of the property and souls of men, for the multiplication of crimes, for the oppression of faith and truth and of the whole Church of God? Oh, Leo! in reality most unfortunate, and sitting on a most perilous throne, I tell you the truth, because I wish you well; for if Bernard felt compassion for his Anastasius at a time when the Roman see, though even then most corrupt, was as yet ruling with better hope than now, why should not we lament, to whom so much further corruption and ruin has been added in three hundred years?

Is it not true that there is nothing under the vast heavens more corrupt, more pestilential, more hateful, than the Court of Rome? She incomparably surpasses the impiety of the Turks, so that in very truth she, who was formerly the gate of heaven, is now a sort of open mouth of hell, and such a mouth as, under the urgent wrath of God, cannot be blocked up; one course alone being left to us wretched men: to call back and save some few, if we can, from that Roman gulf.

Behold, Leo, my father, with what purpose and on what principle it is that I have stormed against that seat of pestilence. I am so far from having felt any rage against your person that I even hoped to gain favor with you and to aid you in your welfare by striking actively and vigorously at that your prison, nay, your hell. For whatever the efforts of all minds can contrive against the confusion of that impious Court will be advantageous to you and to your welfare, and to many others with you. Those who do harm to her are doing your office; those who in every way abhor her are glorifying Christ; in short, those are Christians who are not Romans.

But, to say yet more, even this never entered my heart: to inveigh against the Court of Rome or to dispute at all about her. For, seeing all remedies for her health to be desperate, I looked on her with contempt, and, giving her a bill of divorcement, said to her, "He that is unjust, let him be unjust still; and he that is filthy, let him be filthy still," giving myself up to the peaceful and quiet study of sacred literature, that by this I might be of use to the brethren living about me.

While I was making some advance in these studies, Satan opened his eyes and goaded on his servant John Eccius, that notorious adversary of Christ, by the unchecked lust for fame, to drag me unexpectedly into the arena, trying to catch me in one little word concerning the primacy of the Church of Rome, which had fallen from me in passing. That boastful Thraso, foaming and gnashing his teeth, proclaimed that he would dare all things for the glory of God and for the honor of the holy apostolic seat; and, being puffed up respecting your power, which he was about to misuse, he looked forward with all certainty to victory; seeking to promote, not so much the primacy of Peter, as his own pre-eminence among the theologians of this age; for he thought it would contribute in no slight degree to this, if he were to lead Luther in triumph. The result having proved unfortunate for the sophist, an incredible rage torments him; for he feels that whatever discredit to Rome has arisen through me has been caused by the fault of himself alone.

Suffer me, I pray you, most excellent Leo, both to plead my own cause, and to accuse your true enemies. I believe it is known to you in what way Cardinal Cajetan, your imprudent and unfortunate, nay unfaithful, legate, acted towards me. When, on account of my reverence for your name, I had placed myself and all that was mine in his hands, he did not so act as to establish peace, which he could easily have established by one little word, since I at that time promised to be silent and to make an end of my case, if he would command my adversaries to do the same.

But that man of pride, not content with this agreement, began to justify my adversaries, to give them free licence, and to order me to recant, a thing which was certainly not in his commission. Thus indeed, when the case was in the best position, it came through his vexatious tyranny into a much worse one. Therefore whatever has followed upon this is the fault not of Luther, but entirely of Cajetan, since he did not suffer me to be silent and remain quiet, which at that time I was entreating for with all my might. What more was it my duty to do?

Next came Charles Miltitz, also a nuncio from your Blessedness. He, though he went up and down with much and varied exertion, and omitted nothing which could tend to restore the position of the cause thrown into confusion by the rashness and pride of Cajetan, had difficulty, even with the help of that very illustrious prince the Elector Frederick, in at last bringing about more than one familiar conference with me. In these I again yielded to your great name, and was prepared to keep silence, and to accept as my judge either the Archbishop of Treves, or the Bishop of Naumburg; and thus it was done and concluded.

While this was being done with good hope of success, lo! that other and greater enemy of yours, Eccius, rushed in with his Leipsic disputation, which he had undertaken against Carlstadt, and, having taken up a new question concerning the primacy of the Pope, turned his arms unexpectedly against me, and completely overthrew the plan for peace. Meanwhile Charles Miltitz was waiting, disputations were held, judges were being chosen, but no decision was arrived at. And no wonder! for by the falsehoods, pretences, and arts of Eccius the whole business was brought into such thorough disorder, confusion, and festering soreness, that, whichever way the sentence might lean, a greater conflagration was sure to arise; for he was seeking, not after truth, but after his own credit. In this case too I omitted nothing which it was right that I should do.

I confess that on this occasion no small part of the corruptions of Rome came to light; but, if there was any offence in this, it was the fault of Eccius, who, in taking on him a burden beyond his strength, and in furiously aiming at credit for himself, unveiled to the whole world the disgrace of Rome.

Here is that enemy of yours, Leo, or rather of your Court; by his example alone we may learn that an enemy is not more baneful than a flatterer. For what did he bring about by his flattery, except evils which no king could have brought about? At this day the name of the Court of Rome stinks in the nostrils of the world, the papal authority is growing weak, and its notorious ignorance is evil spoken of.

We should hear none of these things, if Eccius had not disturbed the plans of Miltitz and myself for peace. He feels this clearly enough himself in the indignation he shows, too late and in vain, against the publication of my books. He ought to have reflected on this at the time when he was all mad for renown, and was seeking in your cause nothing but his own objects, and that with the greatest peril to you. The foolish man hoped that, from fear of your name, I should yield and keep silence; for I do not think he presumed on his talents and learning. Now, when he sees that I am very confident and speak aloud, he repents too late of his rashness, and sees—if indeed he does see it—that there is One in heaven who resists the proud, and humbles the presumptuous.

Since then we were bringing about by this disputation nothing but the greater confusion of the cause of Rome, Charles Miltitz for the third time addressed the Fathers of the Order, assembled in chapter, and sought their advice for the settlement of the case, as being now in a most troubled and perilous state. Since, by the favour of God, there was no hope of proceeding against me by force, some of the more noted of their number were sent to me, and begged me at least to show respect to your person and to vindicate in a humble letter both your innocence and my own. They said that the affair was not as yet in a position of extreme hopelessness, if Leo X., in his inborn kindliness, would put his hand to it.

On this I, who have always offered and wished for peace, in order that I might devote myself to calmer and more useful pursuits, and who for this very purpose have acted with so much spirit and vehemence, in order to put down by the strength and impetuosity of my words, as well as of my feelings, men whom I saw to be very far from equal to myself—I, I say, not only gladly yielded, but even accepted it with joy and gratitude, as the greatest kindness and benefit, if you should think it right to satisfy my hopes.

Thus I come, most blessed Father, and in all abasement beseech you to put to your hand, if it is possible, and impose a curb to those flatterers who are enemies of peace, while they pretend peace. But there is no reason, most blessed Father, why any one should assume that I am to utter a recantation, unless he prefers to involve the case in still greater confusion. Moreover, I cannot bear with laws for the interpretation of the word of God, since the word of God, which teaches liberty in all other things, ought not to be bound. Saving these two things, there is nothing which I am not able, and most heartily willing, to do or to suffer. I hate contention; I will challenge no one; in return I wish not to be challenged; but, being challenged, I will not be dumb in the cause of Christ my Master. For your Blessedness will be able by one short and easy word to call these controversies before you and suppress them, and to impose silence and peace on both sides—a word which I have ever longed to hear.

Therefore, Leo, my Father, beware of listening to those sirens who make you out to be not simply a man, but partly a god, so that you can command and require whatever you will. It will not happen so, nor will you prevail. You are the servant of servants, and more than any other man, in a most pitiable and perilous position. Let not those men deceive you who pretend that you are lord of the world; who will not allow any one to be a Christian without your authority; who babble of your having power over heaven, hell, and purgatory. These men are your enemies and are seeking your soul to destroy it, as Isaiah says, "My people, they that call thee blessed are themselves deceiving thee." They are in error who raise you above councils and the universal Church; they are in error who attribute to you alone the right of interpreting Scripture. All these men are seeking to set up their own impieties in the Church under your name, and alas! Satan has gained much through them in the time of your predecessors.

In brief, trust not in any who exalt you, but in those who humiliate you. For this is the judgment of God: "He hath cast down the mighty from their seat, and hath exalted the humble." See how unlike Christ was to His successors, though all will have it that they are His vicars. I fear that in truth very many of them have been in too serious a sense His vicars, for a vicar represents a prince who is absent. Now if a pontiff rules while Christ is absent and does not dwell in his heart, what else is he but a vicar of Christ? And then what is that Church but a multitude without Christ? What indeed is such a vicar but antichrist and an idol? How much more rightly did the Apostles speak, who call themselves servants of a present Christ, not the vicars of an absent one!

Perhaps I am shamelessly bold in seeming to teach so great a head, by whom all men ought to be taught, and from whom, as those plagues of yours boast, the thrones of judges receive their sentence; but I imitate St. Bernard in his book concerning Considerations addressed to Eugenius, a book which ought to be known by heart by every pontiff. I do this, not from any desire to teach, but as a duty, from that simple and faithful solicitude which teaches us to be anxious for all that is safe for our neighbors, and does not allow considerations of worthiness or unworthiness to be entertained, being intent only on the dangers or advantage of others. For since I know that your Blessedness is driven and tossed by the waves at Rome, so that the depths of the sea press on you with infinite perils, and that you are laboring under such a condition of misery that you need even the least help from any the least brother, I do not seem to myself to be acting unsuitably if I forget your majesty till I shall have fulfilled the office of charity. I will not flatter in so serious and perilous a matter; and if in this you do not see that I am your friend and most thoroughly your subject, there is One to see and judge.

In fine, that I may not approach you empty-handed, blessed Father, I bring with me this little treatise, published under your name, as a good omen of the establishment of peace and of good hope. By this you may perceive in what pursuits I should prefer and be able to occupy myself to more profit, if I were allowed, or had been hitherto allowed, by your impious flatterers. It is a small matter, if you look to its exterior, but, unless I mistake, it is a summary of the Christian life put together in small compass, if you apprehend its meaning. I, in my poverty, have no other present to make you, nor do you need anything else than to be enriched by a spiritual gift. I commend myself to your Paternity and Blessedness, whom may the Lord Jesus preserve for ever. Amen.

Wittenberg
6th September, 1520

Concerning Christian Liberty

Christian faith has appeared to many an easy thing; nay, not a few even reckon it among the social virtues, as it were; and this they do because they have not made proof of it experimentally, and have never tasted of what efficacy it is. For it is not possible for any man to write well about it, or to understand well what is rightly written, who has not at some time tasted of its spirit, under the pressure of tribulation; while he who has tasted of it, even to a very small extent, can never write, speak, think, or hear about it sufficiently. For it is a living fountain, springing up into eternal life, as Christ calls it in John 4.

Now, though I cannot boast of my abundance, and though I know how poorly I am furnished, yet I hope that, after having been vexed by various temptations, I have attained some little drop of faith, and that I can speak of this matter, if not with more elegance, certainly with more solidity, than those literal and too subtle disputants who have hitherto discoursed upon it without understanding their own words. That I may open then an easier way for the ignorant—for these alone I am trying to serve—I first lay down these two propositions, concerning spiritual liberty and servitude:

A Christian man is the most free lord of all, and subject to none; a Christian man is the most dutiful servant of all, and subject to every one.

Although these statements appear contradictory, yet, when they are found to agree together, they will make excellently for my purpose. They are both the statements of Paul himself, who says, "Though I be free from all men, yet have I made myself servant unto all" (1 Corinthians 9:19), and "Owe no man anything, but to love one another." (Romans 8:8) Now love is by its own nature dutiful and obedient to the beloved object. Thus even Christ, though Lord of all things, was yet made of a woman; made under the law; at once free and a servant; at once in the form of God and in the form of a servant.

Let us examine the subject on a deeper and less simple principle. Man is composed of a twofold nature, a spiritual and a bodily. As regards the spiritual nature, which they name the soul, he is called the spiritual, inward, new man; as regards the bodily nature, which they name the flesh, he is called the fleshly, outward, old man. The Apostle speaks of this: "Though our outward man perish, yet the inward man is renewed day by day." (2 Corinthians 4:16) The result of this diversity is that in the Scriptures opposing statements are made concerning the same man, the fact being that in the same man these two men are opposed to one another; the flesh lusting against the spirit, and the spirit against the flesh. (Galatians 5:17)

We first approach the subject of the inward man, that we may see by what means a man becomes justified, free, and a true Christian; that is, a spiritual, new, and inward man. It is certain that absolutely none among outward things, under whatever name they may be reckoned, has any influence in producing Christian righteousness or liberty, nor, on the other hand, unrighteousness or slavery. This can be shown by an easy argument.

What can it profit the soul that the body should be in good condition, free, and full of life; that it should eat, drink, and act according to its pleasure; when even the most impious slaves of every kind of vice are prosperous in these matters? Again, what harm can ill-health, bondage, hunger, thirst, or any other outward evil, do to the soul, when even the most pious of men and the freest in the purity of their conscience, are harassed by these things? Neither of these states of things has to do with the liberty or the slavery of the soul.

And so it will profit nothing that the body should be adorned with sacred vestments, or dwell in holy places, or be occupied in sacred offices, or pray, fast, and abstain from certain meats, or do whatever works can be done through the body and in the body. Something widely different will be necessary for the justification and liberty of the soul, since the things I have spoken of can be done by any impious person, and only hypocrites are produced by devotion to these things. On the other hand, it will not at all injure the soul that the body should be clothed in profane raiment, should dwell in profane places, should eat and drink in the ordinary fashion, should not pray aloud, and should leave undone all the things above mentioned, which may be done by hypocrites.

And, to cast everything aside, even speculation, meditations, and whatever things can be performed by the exertions of the soul itself, are of no profit. One thing, and one alone, is necessary for life, justification, and Christian liberty; and that is the most holy word of God, the Gospel of Christ, as He says, "I am the resurrection and the life; he that believeth in Me shall not die eternally" (John 11:25), and also, "If the Son shall make you free, ye shall be free indeed" (John 8:36), and, "Man shall not live by bread alone, but by every word that proceedeth out of the mouth of God." (Matthew 4:4)

Let us therefore hold it for certain and firmly established that the soul can do without everything except the word of God, without which none at all of its wants are provided for. But, having the word, it is rich and wants for nothing, since that is the word of life, of truth, of light, of peace, of justification, of salvation, of joy, of liberty, of wisdom, of virtue, of grace, of glory, and of every good thing. It is on this account that the prophet in a whole Psalm (Psalm 119), and in many other places, sighs for and calls upon the word of God with so many groanings and words.

Again, there is no more cruel stroke of the wrath of God than when He sends a famine of hearing His words (Amos viii. 11), just as there is no greater favor from Him than the sending forth of His word, as it is said, "He sent His word and healed them, and delivered them from their destructions." (Psalm 107:20) Christ was sent for no other office than that of the word; and the order of Apostles, that of bishops, and that of the whole body of the clergy, have been called and instituted for no object but the ministry of the word.

But you will ask, What is this word, and by what means is it to be used, since there are so many words of God? I answer, The Apostle Paul (Romans 1) explains what it is, namely the Gospel of God, concerning His Son, incarnate, suffering, risen, and glorified, through the Spirit, the Sanctifier. To preach Christ is to feed the soul, to justify it, to set it free, and to save it, if it believes the preaching. For faith alone and the efficacious use of the word of God, bring salvation. "If thou shalt confess with thy mouth the Lord Jesus, and shalt believe in thine heart that God hath raised Him from the dead, thou shalt be saved" (Romans 10:9); and again, "Christ is the end of the law for righteousness to every one that believeth" (Romans 4), and "The just shall live by faith." (Romans 1:17) For the word of God cannot be received and honored by any works, but by faith alone. Hence it is clear that as the soul needs the word alone for life and justification, so it is justified by faith alone, and not by any works. For if it could be justified by any other means, it would have no need of the word, nor consequently of faith.

But this faith cannot consist at all with works; that is, if you imagine that you can be justified by those works, whatever they are, along with it. For this would be to halt between two opinions, to worship Baal, and to kiss the hand to him, which is a very great iniquity, as Job says. Therefore, when you begin to believe, you learn at the same time that all that is in you is utterly guilty, sinful, and damnable, according to that saying, "All have sinned, and come short of the glory of God" (Romans 3:23), and also: "There is none righteous, no, not one; they are all gone out of the way; they are together become unprofitable: there is none that doeth good, no, not one." (Romans 3:10-12) When you have learnt this, you will know that Christ is necessary for you, since He has suffered and risen again for you, that, believing on Him, you might by this faith become another man, all your sins being remitted, and you being justified by the merits of another, namely of Christ alone.

Since then this faith can reign only in the inward man, as it is said, "With the heart man believeth unto righteousness" (Romans 10:10); and since it alone justifies, it is evident that by no outward work or labor can the inward man be at all justified, made free, and saved; and that no works whatever have any relation to him. And so, on the other hand, it is solely by impiety and incredulity of heart that he becomes guilty and a slave of sin, deserving condemnation, not by any outward sin or work. Therefore the first care of every Christian ought to be to lay aside all reliance on works, and strengthen his faith alone more and more, and by it grow in the knowledge, not of works, but of Christ Jesus, who has suffered and risen again for him, as Peter teaches (1 Peter 5) when he makes no other work to be a Christian one. Thus Christ, when the Jews asked Him what they should do that they might work the works of God, rejected the multitude of works, with which He saw that they were puffed up, and commanded them one thing only, saying, "This is the work of God: that ye believe on Him whom He hath sent, for Him hath God the Father sealed" (John 6:27, 29).

Hence a right faith in Christ is an incomparable treasure, carrying with it universal salvation and preserving from all evil, as it is said, "He that believeth and is baptized shall be saved; but he that believeth not shall be damned" (Mark xvi. 16). Isaiah, looking to this treasure, predicted, "The consumption decreed shall overflow with righteousness. For the Lord God of hosts shall make a consumption, even determined (verbum abbreviatum et consummans), in the midst of the land" (Isaiah 10:22, 23). As if he said, "Faith, which is the brief and complete fulfilling of the law, will fill those who believe with such righteousness that they will need nothing else for justification." Thus, too, Paul says, "For with the heart man believeth unto righteousness" (Romans 10:10).

But you ask how it can be the fact that faith alone justifies, and affords without works so great a treasure of good things, when so many works, ceremonies, and laws are prescribed to us in the Scriptures? I answer, Before all things bear in mind what I have said:

that faith alone without works justifies, sets free, and saves, as I shall show more clearly below.

Meanwhile it is to be noted that the whole Scripture of God is divided into two parts: precepts and promises. The precepts certainly teach us what is good, but what they teach is not forthwith done. For they show us what we ought to do, but do not give us the power to do it. They were ordained, however, for the purpose of showing man to himself, that through them he may learn his own impotence for good and may despair of his own strength. For this reason they are called the Old Testament, and are so.

For example, "Thou shalt not covet," is a precept by which we are all convicted of sin, since no man can help coveting, whatever efforts to the contrary he may make. In order therefore that he may fulfill the precept, and not covet, he is constrained to despair of himself and to seek elsewhere and through another the help which he cannot find in himself; as it is said, "O Israel, thou hast destroyed thyself; but in Me is thine help." (Hosea 8:9) Now what is done by this one precept is done by all; for all are equally impossible of fulfillment by us.

Now when a man has through the precepts been taught his own impotence, and become anxious by what means he may satisfy the law—for the law must be satisfied, so that no jot or tittle of it may pass away, otherwise he must be hopelessly condemned—then, being truly humbled and brought to nothing in his own eyes, he finds in himself no resource for justification and salvation.

Then comes in that other part of Scripture, the promises of God, which declare the glory of God, and say, "If you wish to fulfill the law, and, as the law requires, not to covet, lo! believe in Christ, in whom are promised to you grace, justification, peace, and liberty." All these things you shall have, if you believe, and shall be without them if you do not believe. For what is impossible for you by all the works of the law, which are many and yet useless, you shall fulfill in an easy and summary way through faith, because God the Father has made everything to depend on faith, so that whosoever has it has all things, and he who has it not has nothing. "For God hath concluded them all in unbelief, that He might have mercy upon all" (Romans 11:32). Thus the promises of God give that which the precepts exact, and fulfill what the law commands; so that all is of God alone, both the precepts and their fulfillment. He alone commands; He alone also fulfills. Hence the promises of God belong to the New Testament; nay, are the New Testament.

Now, since these promises of God are words of holiness, truth, righteousness, liberty, and peace, and are full of universal goodness, the soul, which cleaves to them with a firm faith, is so united to them, nay, thoroughly absorbed by them, that it not only partakes in, but is penetrated and saturated by, all their virtues. For if the touch of Christ was healing, how much more does that most tender spiritual touch, nay, absorption of the word, communicate to the soul all that belongs to the word! In this way therefore the soul, through faith alone, without works, is from the word of God justified, sanctified, endued with truth, peace, and liberty, and filled full with every good thing, and is truly made the child of God, as it is said, "To them gave He power to become the sons of God, even to them that believe on His name." (John 1:12)

From all this it is easy to understand why faith has such great power, and why no good works, nor even all good works put together, can compare with it, since no work can cleave to the word of God or be in the soul. Faith alone and the word reign in it; and such as is the word, such is the soul made by it, just as iron exposed to fire glows

20

like fire, on account of its union with the fire. It is clear then that to a Christian man his faith suffices for everything, and that he has no need of works for justification. But if he has no need of works, neither has he need of the law, and if he has no need of the law, he is certainly free from the law, and the saying is true, "The law is not made for a righteous man." (1 Timothy 1:9) This is that Christian liberty, our faith, the effect of which is, not that we should be careless or lead a bad life, but that no one should need the law or works for justification and salvation.

Let us consider this as the first virtue of faith; and let us look also to the second. This also is an office of faith: that it honors with the utmost veneration and the highest reputation Him in whom it believes, inasmuch as it holds Him to be truthful and worthy of belief. For there is no honor like that reputation of truth and righteousness with which we honor Him in whom we believe. What higher credit can we attribute to any one than truth and righteousness, and absolute goodness? On the other hand, it is the greatest insult to brand any one with the reputation of falsehood and unrighteousness, or to suspect him of these, as we do when we disbelieve him.

Thus the soul, in firmly believing the promises of God, holds Him to be true and righteous; and it can attribute to God no higher glory than the credit of being so. The highest worship of God is to ascribe to Him truth, righteousness, and whatever qualities we must ascribe to one in whom we believe. In doing this the soul shows itself prepared to do His whole will; in doing this it hallows His name, and gives itself up to be dealt with as it may please God. For it cleaves to His promises, and never doubts that He is true, just, and wise, and will do, dispose, and provide for all things in the best way. Is not such a soul, in this its faith, most obedient to God in all things?

What commandment does there remain which has not been amply fulfilled by such an obedience? What fulfillment can be more full than universal obedience? Now this is not accomplished by works, but by faith alone.

On the other hand, what greater rebellion, impiety, or insult to God can there be, than not to believe His promises? What else is this, than either to make God a liar, or to doubt His truth—that is, to attribute truth to ourselves, but to God falsehood and levity? In doing this, is not a man denying God and setting himself up as an idol in his own heart? What then can works, done in such a state of impiety, profit us, were they even angelic or apostolic works? Rightly hath God shut up all, not in wrath nor in lust, but in unbelief, in order that those who pretend that they are fulfilling the law by works of purity and benevolence (which are social and human virtues) may not presume that they will therefore be saved, but, being included in the sin of unbelief, may either seek mercy, or be justly condemned.

But when God sees that truth is ascribed to Him, and that in the faith of our hearts He is honored with all the honor of which He is worthy, then in return He honors us on account of that faith, attributing to us truth and righteousness. For faith does truth and righteousness in rendering to God what is His; and therefore in return God gives glory to our righteousness. It is true and righteous that God is true and righteous; and to confess this and ascribe these attributes to Him, this it is to be true and righteous. Thus He says, "Them that honor Me I will honor, and they that despise Me shall be lightly esteemed." (1 Samuel 2:30) And so Paul says that Abraham's faith was imputed to him for righteousness, because by it he gave glory to God; and that to us also, for the same reason, it shall be imputed for righteousness, if we believe. (Romans 4)

The third incomparable grace of faith is this: that it unites the soul to Christ, as the wife to the husband, by which mystery, as the Apostle teaches, Christ and the soul are made one flesh. Now if they are one flesh, and if a true marriage—nay, by far the most perfect of all marriages—is accomplished between them (for human marriages are but feeble types of this one great marriage), then it follows that all they have becomes theirs in common, as well good things as evil things; so that whatsoever Christ possesses, that the believing soul may take to itself and boast of as its own, and whatever belongs to the soul, that Christ claims as His.

If we compare these possessions, we shall see how inestimable is the gain. Christ is full of grace, life, and salvation; the soul is full of sin, death, and condemnation. Let faith step in, and then sin, death, and hell will belong to Christ, and grace, life, and salvation to the soul. For, if He is a Husband, He must needs take to Himself that which is His wife's, and at the same time, impart to His wife that which is His. For, in giving her His own body and Himself, how can He but give her all that is His? And, in taking to Himself the body of His wife, how can He but take to Himself all that is hers?

In this is displayed the delightful sight, not only of communion, but of a prosperous warfare, of victory, salvation, and redemption. For, since Christ is God and man, and is such a Person as neither has sinned, nor dies, nor is condemned, nay, cannot sin, die, or be condemned, and since His righteousness, life, and salvation are invincible, eternal, and almighty,—when I say, such a Person, by the wedding-ring of faith, takes a share in the sins, death, and hell of His wife, nay, makes them His own, and deals with them no otherwise than as if they were His, and as if He Himself had sinned; and when He suffers, dies, and descends to hell, that He may overcome all things, and since sin, death, and hell cannot swallow Him up, they must needs be swallowed up by Him in stupendous conflict. For His righteousness rises above the sins of all men; His life is more powerful than all death; His salvation is more unconquerable than all hell.

Thus the believing soul, by the pledge of its faith in Christ, becomes free from all sin, fearless of death, safe from hell, and endowed with the eternal righteousness, life, and salvation of its Husband Christ. Thus He presents to Himself a glorious bride, without spot or wrinkle, cleansing her with the washing of water by the word; that is, by faith in the word of life, righteousness, and salvation. Thus He betroths her unto Himself "in faithfulness, in righteousness, and in judgment, and in loving-kindness, and in mercies." (Hosea 2:19, 20).

Who then can value highly enough these royal nuptials? Who can comprehend the riches of the glory of this grace? Christ, that rich and pious Husband, takes as a wife a needy and impious harlot, redeeming her from all her evils and supplying her with all His good things. It is impossible now that her sins should destroy her, since they have been laid upon Christ and swallowed up in Him, and since she has in her Husband Christ a righteousness which she may claim as her own, and which she can set up with confidence against all her sins, against death and hell, saying, "If I have sinned, my Christ, in whom I believe, has not sinned; all mine is His, and all His is mine," as it is written, "My beloved is mine, and I am His." (Canticle 2:16) This is what Paul says: "Thanks be to God, which giveth us the victory through our Lord Jesus Christ," victory over sin and death, as he says, "The sting of death is sin, and the strength of sin is the law" (1 Corinthians 15:56, 57)

From all this you will again understand why so much importance is attributed to faith, so that it alone can fulfill the law and justify without any works. For you see that the First Commandment, which says, "Thou shalt worship one God only," is fulfilled by faith alone. If you were nothing but good works from the soles of your feet to the crown of your head, you would not be worshiping God, nor fulfilling the First Commandment, since it is impossible to worship God without ascribing to Him the glory of truth and of universal goodness, as it ought in truth to be ascribed. Now this is not done by works, but only by faith of heart. It is not by working, but by believing, that we glorify God, and confess Him to be true. On this ground faith alone is the righteousness of a Christian man, and the fulfilling of all the commandments. For to him who fulfills the first the task of fulfilling all the rest is easy.

Works, since they are irrational things, cannot glorify God, although they may be done to the glory of God, if faith be present. But at present we are inquiring, not into the quality of the works done, but into him who does them, who glorifies God, and brings forth good works. This is faith of heart, the head and the substance of all our righteousness. Hence that is a blind and perilous doctrine which teaches that the commandments are fulfilled by works. The commandments must have been fulfilled previous to any good works, and good works follow their fulfillment, as we shall see.

But, that we may have a wider view of that grace which our inner man has in Christ, we must know that in the Old Testament God sanctified to Himself every first-born male. The birthright was of great value, giving a superiority over the rest by the double honor of priesthood and kingship. For the first-born brother was priest and lord of all the rest.

Under this figure was fore-shown Christ, the true and only First-born of God the Father and of the Virgin Mary, and a true King and Priest, not in a fleshly and earthly sense. For His kingdom is not of this world; it is in heavenly and spiritual things that He reigns and acts as Priest; and these are righteousness, truth, wisdom, peace, salvation, etc. Not but that all things, even those of earth and hell, are subject to Him—for otherwise how could He defend and save us from them?—but it is not in these, nor by these, that His kingdom stands.

So, too, His priesthood does not consist in the outward display of vestments and gestures, as did the human priesthood of Aaron and our ecclesiastical priesthood at this day, but in spiritual things, wherein, in His invisible office, He intercedes for us with God in heaven, and there offers Himself, and performs all the duties of a priest, as Paul describes Him to the Hebrews under the figure of Melchizedek. Nor does He only pray and intercede for us; He also teaches us inwardly in the spirit with the living teachings of His Spirit. Now these are the two special offices of a priest, as is figured to us in the case of fleshly priests by visible prayers and sermons.

As Christ by His birthright has obtained these two dignities, so He imparts and communicates them to every believer in Him, under that law of matrimony of which we have spoken above, by which all that is the husband's is also the wife's. Hence all we who believe on Christ are kings and priests in Christ, as it is said, "Ye are a chosen generation, a royal priesthood, a holy nation, a peculiar people, that ye should show forth the praises of Him who hath called you out of darkness into His marvelous light." (1 Peter 2:9)

These two things stand thus. First, as regards kingship, every Christian is by faith so exalted above all things that, in spiritual power, he is completely lord of all things, so that nothing whatever can do him any hurt; yea, all things are subject to him, and are compelled to be subservient to his salvation. Thus Paul says, "All things work together for good to them who are the called" (Romans 8:28), and also, "Whether life, or death, or things present, or things to come, all are yours; and ye are Christ's." (1 Corinthians 3:22, 23).

Not that in the sense of corporeal power any one among Christians has been appointed to possess and rule all things, according to the mad and senseless idea of certain ecclesiastics. That is the office of kings, princes, and men upon earth. In the experience of life we see that we are subjected to all things, and suffer many things, even death. Yea, the more of a Christian any man is, to so many the more evils, sufferings, and deaths is he subject, as we see in the first place in Christ the First-born, and in all His holy brethren.

This is a spiritual power, which rules in the midst of enemies, and is powerful in the midst of distresses. And this is nothing else than that strength is made perfect in my weakness, and that I can turn all things to the profit of my salvation; so that even the cross and death are compelled to serve me and to work together for my salvation. This is a lofty and eminent dignity, a true and almighty dominion, a spiritual empire, in which there is nothing so good, nothing so bad, as not to work together for my good, if only I believe. And yet there is nothing of which I have need—for faith alone suffices for my salvation—unless that in it faith may exercise the power and empire of its liberty. This is the inestimable power and liberty of Christians.

Nor are we only kings and the freest of all men, but also priests for ever, a dignity far higher than kingship, because by that priesthood we are worthy to appear before God, to pray for others, and to teach one another mutually the things which are of God. For these are the duties of priests, and they cannot possibly be permitted to any unbeliever. Christ has obtained for us this favor, if we believe in Him: that just as we are His brethren and co-heirs and fellow-kings with Him, so we should be also fellow-priests with Him, and venture with confidence, through the spirit of faith, to come into the presence of God, and cry, "Abba, Father!" and to pray for one another, and to do all things which we see done and figured in the visible and corporeal office of priesthood. But to an unbelieving person nothing renders service or work for good. He himself is in servitude to all things, and all things turn out for evil to him, because he uses all things in an impious way for his own advantage, and not for the glory of God. And thus he is not a priest, but a profane person, whose prayers are turned into sin, nor does he ever appear in the presence of God, because God does not hear sinners.

Who then can comprehend the loftiness of that Christian dignity which, by its royal power, rules over all things, even over death, life, and sin, and, by its priestly glory, is all-powerful with God, since God does what He Himself seeks and wishes, as it is written, "He will fulfill the desire of them that fear Him; He also will hear their cry, and will save them"? (Psalm 145:19) This glory certainly cannot be attained by any works, but by faith only.

From these considerations any one may clearly see how a Christian man is free from all things; so that he needs no works in order to be justified and saved, but receives these gifts in abundance from faith alone. Nay, were he so foolish as to pretend to be justified, set free, saved, and made a Christian, by means of any good work, he would immediately lose faith, with all its benefits. Such folly is prettily represented in the fable where a dog, running along in the water and carrying in his mouth a real piece of meat, is deceived by the reflection of the meat in the water, and, in trying with open mouth to seize it, loses the meat and its image at the same time.

Here you will ask, "If all who are in the Church are priests, by what character are those whom we now call priests to be distinguished from the laity?" I reply, By the use of these words, "priest," "clergy," "spiritual person," "ecclesiastic," an injustice has been done, since they have been transferred from the remaining body of Christians to those few who are now, by hurtful custom, called ecclesiastics. For Holy Scripture makes no distinction between them, except that those who are now boastfully called popes, bishops, and lords, it calls ministers, servants, and stewards, who are to serve the rest in the ministry of the word, for teaching the faith of Christ and the liberty of believers. For though it is true that we are all equally priests, yet we cannot, nor, if we could, ought we all to, minister and teach publicly. Thus Paul says, "Let a man so account of us as of the ministers of Christ and stewards of the mysteries of God." (1 Corinthians 4:1)

This bad system has now issued in such a pompous display of power and such a terrible tyranny that no earthly government can be compared to it, as if the laity were something else than Christians. Through this perversion of things it has happened that the knowledge of Christian grace, of faith, of liberty, and altogether of Christ, has utterly perished, and has been succeeded by an intolerable bondage to human works and laws; and, according to the Lamentations of Jeremiah, we have become the slaves of the vilest men on earth, who abuse our misery to all the disgraceful and ignominious purposes of their own will.

Returning to the subject which we had begun, I think it is made clear by these considerations that it is not sufficient, nor a Christian course, to preach the works, life, and words of Christ in a historic manner, as facts which it suffices to know as an example how to frame our life, as do those who are now held the best preachers, and much less so to keep silence altogether on these things and to teach in their stead the laws of men and the decrees of the Fathers. There are now not a few persons who preach and read about Christ with the object of moving the human affections to sympathize with Christ, to indignation against the Jews, and other childish and womanish absurdities of that kind.

Now preaching ought to have the object of promoting faith in Him, so that He may not only be Christ, but a Christ for you and for me, and that what is said of Him, and what He is called, may work in us. And this faith is produced and is maintained by preaching why Christ came, what He has brought us and given to us, and to what profit and advantage He is to be received. This is done when the Christian liberty which we have from Christ Himself is rightly taught, and we are shown in what manner all we Christians are kings and priests, and how we are lords of all things, and may be confident that whatever we do in the presence of God is pleasing and acceptable to Him.

Whose heart would not rejoice in its inmost core at hearing these things? Whose heart, on receiving so great a consolation, would not become sweet with the love of Christ, a love to which it can never attain by any laws or works? Who can injure such a heart, or make it afraid? If the consciousness of sin or the horror of death rush in upon it, it is prepared to hope in the Lord, and is fearless of such evils, and undisturbed, until it shall look down upon its enemies. For it believes that the righteousness of Christ is its own, and that its sin is no longer its own, but that of Christ; but, on account of its faith in Christ, all its sin must needs be swallowed up from before the face of the righteousness of Christ, as I have said above. It learns, too, with the Apostle, to scoff at death and sin, and to say, "O death, where is thy sting? O grave, where is thy victory? The sting of death is sin, and the strength of sin is the law. But thanks be to God, which giveth us the victory through our Lord Jesus Christ." (1 Corinthians 15:55-57) For death is swallowed up in victory, not only the victory of Christ, but ours also, since by faith it becomes ours, and in it we too conquer.

Let it suffice to say this concerning the inner man and its liberty, and concerning that righteousness of faith which needs neither laws nor good works; nay, they are even hurtful to it, if any one pretends to be justified by them.

And now let us turn to the other part: to the outward man. Here we shall give an answer to all those who, taking offence at the word of faith and at what I have asserted, say, "If faith does everything, and by itself suffices for justification, why then are good works commanded? Are we then to take our ease and do no works, content with faith?" Not so, impious men, I reply; not so. That would indeed really be the case, if we were thoroughly and completely inner and spiritual persons; but that will not happen until the last day, when the dead shall be raised. As long as we live in the flesh, we are but beginning and making advances in that which shall be completed in a future life. On this account the Apostle calls that which we have in this life the firstfruits of the Spirit. (Romans 8:23) In future we shall have the tenths, and the fullness of the Spirit. To this part belongs the fact I have stated before: that the Christian is the servant of all and subject to all. For in that part in which he is free he does no works, but in that in which he is a servant he does all works. Let us see on what principle this is so.

Although, as I have said, inwardly, and according to the spirit, a man is amply enough justified by faith, having all that he requires to have, except that this very faith and abundance ought to increase from day to day, even till the future life, still he remains in this mortal life upon earth, in which it is necessary that he should rule his own body and have intercourse with men. Here then works begin; here he must not take his ease; here he must give heed to exercise his body by fastings, watchings, labor, and other regular discipline, so that it may be subdued to the spirit, and obey and conform itself to the inner man and faith, and not rebel against them nor hinder them, as is its nature to do if it is not kept under. For the inner man, being conformed to God and created after the image of God through faith, rejoices and delights itself in Christ, in whom such blessings have been conferred on it, and hence has only this task before it: to serve God with joy and for nought in free love.

But in doing this he comes into collision with that contrary will in his own flesh, which is striving to serve the world and to seek its own gratification. This the spirit of faith cannot and will not bear, but applies itself with cheerfulness and zeal to keep it down and restrain it, as Paul says, "I delight in the law of God after the inward man; but I see another law in my members, warring against the law of my mind and bringing me into captivity to the law of sin" (Romans 7:22, 23), and again, "I keep under my body, and bring it unto subjection, lest that by any means, when I have preached to others, I myself should be a castaway" (1 Corinthians 9:27), and "They that are Christ's have crucified the flesh, with the affections and lusts." (Galatians 5:24)

These works, however, must not be done with any notion that by them a man can be justified before God—for faith, which alone is righteousness before God, will not bear with this false notion—but solely with this purpose: that the body may be brought into subjection, and be purified from its evil lusts, so that our eyes may be turned only to purging away those lusts. For when the soul has been cleansed by faith and made to love God, it would have all things to be cleansed in like manner, and especially its own body, so that all things might unite with it in the love and praise of God. Thus it comes that, from the requirements of his own body, a man cannot take his ease, but is compelled on its account to do many good works, that he may bring it into subjection. Yet these works are not the means of his justification before God; he does them out of disinterested love to the service of God; looking to no other end than to do what is well-pleasing to Him whom he desires to obey most dutifully in all things.

On this principle every man may easily instruct himself in what measure, and with what distinctions, he ought to chasten his own body. He will fast, watch, and labor, just as much as he sees to suffice for keeping down the wantonness and concupiscence of the body. But those who pretend to be justified by works are looking, not to the mortification of their lusts, but only to the works themselves; thinking that, if they can accomplish as many works and as great ones as possible, all is well with them, and they are justified. Sometimes they even injure their brain, and extinguish nature, or at least make it useless. This is enormous folly, and ignorance of Christian life and faith, when a man seeks, without faith, to be justified and saved by works.

To make what we have said more easily understood, let us set it forth under a figure. The works of a Christian man, who is justified and saved by his faith out of the pure and unbought mercy of God, ought to be regarded in the same light as would have been those of Adam and Eve in paradise and of all their posterity if they had not sinned. Of them it is said, "The Lord God took the man and put him into the garden of Eden to dress it and to keep it." (Genesis 2:15) Now Adam had been created by God just and righteous, so that he could not have needed to be justified and made righteous by keeping the garden and working in it; but, that he might not be unemployed, God gave him the business of keeping and cultivating paradise. These would have indeed been works of perfect freedom, being done for no object but that of pleasing God, and not in order to obtain justification, which he already had to the full, and which would have been innate in us all.

So it is with the works of a believer. Being by his faith replaced afresh in paradise and created anew, he does not need works for his justification, but that he may not be idle, but may exercise his own body and preserve it. His works are to be done freely, with the sole object of pleasing God. Only we are not yet fully created anew in perfect faith and love; these require to be increased, not, however, through works, but through themselves.

A bishop, when he consecrates a church, confirms children, or performs any other duty of his office, is not consecrated as bishop by these works; nay, unless he had been previously consecrated as bishop, not one of those works would have any validity; they would be foolish, childish, and ridiculous. Thus a Christian, being consecrated by his faith, does good works; but he is not by these works made a more sacred person, or more a Christian. That is the effect of faith alone; nay, unless he were previously a believer and a Christian, none of his works would have any value at all; they would really be impious and damnable sins.

True, then, are these two sayings: "Good works do not make a good man, but a good man does good works"; "Bad works do not make a bad man, but a bad man does bad works." Thus it is always necessary that the substance or person should be good before any good works can be done, and that good works should follow and proceed from a good person. As Christ says, "A good tree cannot bring forth evil fruit, neither can a corrupt tree bring forth good fruit." (Matthew 7:18) Now it is clear that the fruit does not bear the tree, nor does the tree grow on the fruit; but, on the contrary, the trees bear the fruit, and the fruit grows on the trees.

As then trees must exist before their fruit, and as the fruit does not make the tree either good or bad, but on the contrary, a tree of either kind produces fruit of the same kind, so must first the person of the man be good or bad before he can do either a good or a bad work; and his works do not make him bad or good, but he himself makes his works either bad or good.

We may see the same thing in all handicrafts. A bad or good house does not make a bad or good builder, but a good or bad builder makes a good or bad house. And in general no work makes the workman such as it is itself; but the workman makes the work such as he is himself. Such is the case, too, with the works of men. Such as the man himself is, whether in faith or in unbelief, such is his work: good if it be done in faith; bad if in unbelief. But the converse is not true that, such as the work is, such the man becomes in faith or in unbelief. For as works do not make a believing man, so neither do they make a justified man; but faith, as it makes a man a believer and justified, so also it makes his works good.

Since then works justify no man, but a man must be justified before he can do any good work, it is most evident that it is faith alone which, by the mere mercy of God through Christ, and by means of His word, can worthily and sufficiently justify and save the person;

and that a Christian man needs no work, no law, for his salvation; for by faith he is free from all law, and in perfect freedom does gratuitously all that he does, seeking nothing either of profit or of salvation—since by the grace of God he is already saved and rich in all things through his faith—but solely that which is well-pleasing to God.

So, too, no good work can profit an unbeliever to justification and salvation; and, on the other hand, no evil work makes him an evil and condemned person, but that unbelief, which makes the person and the tree bad, makes his works evil and condemned. Wherefore, when any man is made good or bad, this does not arise from his works, but from his faith or unbelief, as the wise man says, "The beginning of sin is to fall away from God"; that is, not to believe. Paul says, "He that cometh to God must believe" (Hebrews 11:6); and Christ says the same thing: "Either make the tree good and his fruit good; or else make the tree corrupt, and his fruit corrupt." (Matthew 12:33),—as much as to say, He who wishes to have good fruit will begin with the tree, and plant a good one; even so he who wishes to do good works must begin, not by working, but by believing, since it is this which makes the person good. For nothing makes the person good but faith, nor bad but unbelief.

It is certainly true that, in the sight of men, a man becomes good or evil by his works; but here "becoming" means that it is thus shown and recognized who is good or evil, as Christ says, "By their fruits ye shall know them" (Matt. vii. 20). But all this stops at appearances and externals; and in this matter very many deceive themselves, when they presume to write and teach that we are to be justified by good works, and meanwhile make no mention even of faith, walking in their own ways, ever deceived and deceiving, going from bad to worse, blind leaders of the blind, wearying themselves with many works, and yet never attaining to true righteousness, of whom Paul says, "Having a form of godliness, but denying the power thereof, ever learning and never able to come to the knowledge of the truth." (2 Timothy 3:5, 7)

He then who does not wish to go astray, with these blind ones, must look further than to the works of the law or the doctrine of works; nay, must turn away his sight from works, and look to the person, and to the manner in which it may be justified. Now it is justified and saved, not by works or laws, but by the word of God—that is, by the promise of His grace—so that the glory may be to the Divine majesty, which has saved us who believe, not by works of righteousness which we have done, but according to His mercy, by the word of His grace.

From all this it is easy to perceive on what principle good works are to be cast aside or embraced, and by what rule all teachings put forth concerning works are to be understood. For if works are brought forward as grounds of justification, and are done under the false persuasion that we can pretend to be justified by them, they lay on us the yoke of necessity, and extinguish liberty along with faith, and by this very addition to their use they become no longer good, but really worthy of condemnation. For such works are not free, but blaspheme the grace of God, to which alone it belongs to justify and save through faith. Works cannot accomplish this, and yet, with impious presumption, through our folly, they take it on themselves to do so; and thus break in with violence upon the office and glory of grace.

We do not then reject good works; nay, we embrace them and teach them in the highest degree. It is not on their own account that we condemn them, but on account of this impious addition to them and the perverse notion of seeking justification by them. These things cause them to be only good in outward show, but in reality not good, since by them men are deceived and deceive others, like ravening wolves in sheep's clothing.

Now this leviathan, this perverted notion about works, is invincible when sincere faith is wanting. For those sanctified doers of works cannot but hold it till faith, which destroys it, comes and reigns in the heart. Nature cannot expel it by her own power; nay, cannot even see it for what it is, but considers it as a most holy will. And when custom steps in besides, and strengthens this pravity of nature, as has happened by means of impious teachers, then the evil is incurable, and leads astray multitudes to irreparable ruin. Therefore, though it is good to preach and write about penitence, confession, and satisfaction, yet if we stop there, and do not go on to teach faith, such teaching is without doubt deceitful and devilish. For Christ, speaking by His servant John, not only said, "Repent ye," but added, "for the kingdom of heaven is at hand." (Matthew 3:2)

For not one word of God only, but both, should be preached; new and old things should be brought out of the treasury, as well the voice of the law as the word of grace. The voice of the law should be brought forward, that men may be terrified and brought to a knowledge of their sins, and thence be converted to penitence and to a better manner of life. But we must not stop here; that would be to wound only and not to bind up, to strike and not to heal, to kill and not to make alive, to bring down to hell and not to bring back, to humble and not to exalt. Therefore the word of grace and of the promised remission of sin must also be preached, in order to teach and set up faith, since without that word contrition, penitence, and all other duties, are performed and taught in vain.

There still remain, it is true, preachers of repentance and grace, but they do not explain the law and the promises of God to such an end, and in such a spirit, that men may learn whence repentance and grace are to come. For repentance comes from the law of God, but faith or grace from the promises of God, as it is said, "Faith cometh by hearing, and hearing by the word of God" (Romans 10:17), whence it comes that a man, when humbled and brought to the knowledge of himself by the threatenings and terrors of the law, is consoled and raised up by faith in the Divine promise. Thus "weeping may endure for a night, but joy cometh in the morning" (Psalm 3:5). Thus much we say concerning works in general, and also concerning those which the Christian practices with regard to his own body.

Lastly, we will speak also of those works which he performs towards his neighbor. For man does not live for himself alone in this mortal body, in order to work on its account, but also for all men on earth; nay, he lives only for others, and not for himself. For it is to this end that he brings his own body into subjection, that he may be able to serve others more sincerely and more freely, as Paul says, "None of us liveth to himself, and no man dieth to himself. For whether we live, we live unto the Lord; and whether we die, we die unto the Lord." (Romans 14:7, 8). Thus it is impossible that he should take his ease in this life, and not work for the good of his neighbors, since he must needs speak, act, and converse among men, just as Christ was made in the likeness of men and found in fashion as a man, and had His conversation among men.

Yet a Christian has need of none of these things for justification and salvation, but in all his works he ought to entertain this view and look only to this object—that he may serve and be useful to others in all that he does; having nothing before his eyes but the necessities and the advantage of his neighbor. Thus the Apostle commands us to work with our own hands, that we may have to give to those that need. He might have said, that we may support ourselves; but he tells us to give to those that need. It is the part of a Christian to take care of his own body for the very purpose that, by its soundness and well-being, he may be enabled to labor, and to acquire and preserve property, for the aid of those who are in want, that thus the stronger member may serve the weaker member, and we may be children of God, thoughtful and busy one for another, bearing one another's burdens, and so fulfilling the law of Christ.

Here is the truly Christian life, here is faith really working by love, when a man applies himself with joy and love to the works of that freest servitude in which he serves others voluntarily and for nought, himself abundantly satisfied in the fullness and riches of his own faith.

Thus, when Paul had taught the Philippians how they had been made rich by that faith in Christ in which they had obtained all things, he teaches them further in these words: "If there be therefore any consolation in Christ, if any comfort of love, if any fellowship of the Spirit, if any bowels and mercies, fulfill ye my joy, that ye be like-minded, having the same love, being of one accord, of one mind. Let nothing be done through strife or vainglory; but in lowliness of mind let each esteem other better than themselves. Look not every man on his own things, but every man also on the things of others." (Philippians 2:1-4)

In this we see clearly that the Apostle lays down this rule for a Christian life: that all our works should be directed to the advantage of others, since every Christian has such abundance through his faith that all his other works and his whole life remain over and above wherewith to serve and benefit his neighbor of spontaneous goodwill.

To this end he brings forward Christ as an example, saying, "Let this mind be in you, which was also in Christ Jesus, who, being in the form of God, thought it not robbery to be equal with God, but made Himself of no reputation, and took upon Him the form of a servant, and was made in the likeness of men; and being found in fashion as a man, He humbled Himself, and became obedient unto death." (Philippians 2:5-8) This most wholesome saying of the Apostle has been darkened to us by men who, totally misunderstanding the expressions "form of God," "form of a servant," "fashion," "likeness of men," have transferred them to the natures of Godhead and manhood. Paul's meaning is this: Christ, when He was full of the form of God and abounded in all good things, so that He had no need of works or sufferings to be just and saved—for all these things He had from the very beginning—yet was not puffed up with these things, and did not raise Himself above us and arrogate to Himself power over us, though He might lawfully have done so, but, on the contrary, so acted in laboring, working, suffering, and dying, as to be like the rest of men, and no otherwise than a man in fashion and in conduct, as if He were in want of all things and had nothing of the form of God; and yet all this He did for our sakes, that He might serve us, and that all the works He should do under that form of a servant might become ours.

Thus a Christian, like Christ his Head, being full and in abundance through his faith, ought to be content with this form of God, obtained by faith; except that, as I have said, he ought to increase this faith till it be perfected. For this faith is his life, justification, and salvation, preserving his person itself and making it pleasing to God, and bestowing on him all that Christ has, as I have said above, and as Paul affirms: "The life which I now live in the flesh I live by the faith of the Son of God." (Galatians 2:20) Though he is thus free from all works, yet he ought to empty himself of this liberty, take on him the form of a servant, be made in the likeness of men, be found in fashion as a man, serve, help, and in every way act towards his neighbor as he sees that God through Christ has acted and is acting towards him. All this he should do freely, and with regard to nothing but the good pleasure of God, and he should reason thus:

Lo! my God, without merit on my part, of His pure and free mercy, has given to me, an unworthy, condemned, and contemptible creature all the riches of justification and salvation in Christ, so that I no longer am in want of anything, except of faith to believe that this is so. For such a Father, then, who has overwhelmed me with these inestimable riches of His, why should I not freely, cheerfully, and with my whole heart, and from voluntary zeal, do all that I know will be pleasing to Him and acceptable in His sight? I will therefore give myself as a sort of Christ, to my neighbor, as Christ has given Himself to me; and will do nothing in this life except what I see will be needful, advantageous, and wholesome for my neighbor, since by faith I abound in all good things in Christ.

Thus from faith flow forth love and joy in the Lord, and from love a cheerful, willing, free spirit, disposed to serve our neighbor voluntarily, without taking any account of gratitude or ingratitude, praise or blame, gain or loss. Its object is not to lay men under obligations, nor does it distinguish between friends and enemies, or look to gratitude or ingratitude, but most freely and willingly spends itself and its goods, whether it loses them through ingratitude, or gains goodwill. For thus did its Father, distributing all things to all men abundantly and freely, making His sun to rise upon the just and the unjust. Thus, too, the child does and endures nothing except from the free joy with which it delights through Christ in God, the Giver of such great gifts.

You see, then, that, if we recognize those great and precious gifts, as Peter says, which have been given to us, love is quickly diffused in our hearts through the Spirit, and by love we are made free, joyful, all-powerful, active workers, victors over all our tribulations, servants to our neighbor, and nevertheless lords of all things. But, for those who do not recognize the good things given to them through Christ, Christ has been born in vain; such persons walk by works, and will never attain the taste and feeling of these great things. Therefore just as our neighbor is in want, and has need of our abundance, so we too in the sight of God were in want, and had need of His mercy. And as our heavenly Father has freely helped us in Christ, so ought we freely to help our neighbor by our body and works, and each should become to other a sort of Christ, so that we may be mutually Christs, and that the same Christ may be in all of us; that is, that we may be truly Christians.

Who then can comprehend the riches and glory of the Christian life? It can do all things, has all things, and is in want of nothing; is lord over sin, death, and hell, and at the same time is the obedient and useful servant of all. But alas! it is at this day unknown throughout the world; it is neither preached nor sought after, so that we are quite ignorant about our own name, why we are and are called Christians. We are certainly called so from Christ, who is not absent, but dwells among us—provided, that is, that we believe in Him and are reciprocally and mutually one the Christ of the other, doing to our neighbor as Christ does to us. But now, in the doctrine of men, we are taught only to seek after merits, rewards, and things which are already ours, and we have made of Christ a taskmaster far more severe than Moses.

The Blessed Virgin beyond all others, affords us an example of the same faith, in that she was purified according to the law of Moses, and like all other women, though she was bound by no such law and had no need of purification. Still she submitted to the law voluntarily and of free love, making herself like the rest of women, that she might not offend or throw contempt on them. She was not justified by doing this; but, being already justified, she did it freely and gratuitously. Thus ought our works too to be done, and not in order to be justified by them; for, being first justified by faith, we ought to do all our works freely and cheerfully for the sake of others.

St. Paul circumcised his disciple Timothy, not because he needed circumcision for his justification, but that he might not offend or contemn those Jews, weak in the faith, who had not yet been able to comprehend the liberty of faith. On the other hand, when they contemned liberty and urged that circumcision was necessary for justification, he resisted them, and would not allow Titus to be circumcised. For, as he would not offend or contemn any one's weakness in faith, but yielded for the time to their will, so, again, he would not have the liberty of faith offended or contemned by hardened self-justifiers, but walked in a middle path, sparing the weak for the time, and always resisting the hardened, that he might convert all to the liberty of faith. On the same principle we ought to act, receiving those that are weak in the faith, but boldly resisting these hardened teachers of works, of whom we shall hereafter speak at more length.

Christ also, when His disciples were asked for the tribute money, asked of Peter whether the children of a king were not free from taxes. Peter agreed to this; yet Jesus commanded him to go to the sea, saying, "Lest we should offend them, go thou to the sea, and cast a hook, and take up the fish that first cometh up; and when thou hast opened his mouth thou shalt find a piece of money; that take, and give unto them for Me and thee." (Matthew 17:27)

This example is very much to our purpose; for here Christ calls Himself and His disciples free men and children of a King, in want of nothing; and yet He voluntarily submits and pays the tax. Just as far, then, as this work was necessary or useful to Christ for justification or salvation, so far do all His other works or those of His disciples avail for justification. They are really free and subsequent to justification, and only done to serve others and set them an example.

Such are the works which Paul inculcated, that Christians should be subject to principalities and powers and ready to every good work (Titus 3:1), not that they may be justified by these things—for they are already justified by faith—but that in liberty of spirit they may thus be the servants of others and subject to powers, obeying their will out of gratuitous love.

Such, too, ought to have been the works of all colleges, monasteries, and priests; every one doing the works of his own profession and state of life, not in order to be justified by them, but in order to bring his own body into subjection, as an example to others, who themselves also need to keep under their bodies, and also in order to accommodate himself to the will of others, out of free love. But we must always guard most carefully against any vain confidence or presumption of being justified, gaining merit, or being saved by these works, this being the part of faith alone, as I have so often said.

Any man possessing this knowledge may easily keep clear of danger among those innumerable commands and precepts of the Pope, of bishops, of monasteries, of churches, of princes, and of magistrates, which some foolish pastors urge on us as being necessary for justification and salvation, calling them precepts of the Church, when they are not so at all. For the Christian freeman will speak thus: I will fast, I will pray, I will do this or that which is commanded me by men, not as having any need of these things for justification or salvation, but that I may thus comply with the will of the Pope, of the bishop, of such a community or such a magistrate, or of my neighbor as an example to him; for this cause I will do and suffer all things, just as Christ did and suffered much more for me, though He needed not at all to do so on His own account, and made Himself for my sake under the law, when He was not under the law. And although tyrants may do me violence or wrong in requiring obedience to these things, yet it will not hurt me to do them, so long as they are not done against God.

From all this every man will be able to attain a sure judgment and faithful discrimination between all works and laws, and to know who are blind and foolish pastors, and who are true and good ones. For whatsoever work is not directed to the sole end either of keeping under the body, or of doing service to our neighbor—provided he require nothing contrary to the will of God—is no good or Christian work. Hence I greatly fear that at this day few or no colleges, monasteries, altars, or ecclesiastical functions are Christian ones; and the same may be said of fasts and special prayers to certain saints. I fear that in all these nothing is being sought but what is already ours; while we fancy that by these things our sins are purged away and salvation is attained, and thus utterly do away with Christian liberty. This comes from ignorance of Christian faith and liberty.

This ignorance and this crushing of liberty are diligently promoted by the teaching of very many blind pastors, who stir up and urge the people to a zeal for these things, praising them and puffing them up with their indulgences, but never teaching faith. Now I would advise you, if you have any wish to pray, to fast, or to make foundations in churches, as they call it, to take care not to do so with the object of gaining any advantage, either temporal or eternal. You will thus wrong your faith, which alone bestows all things on you, and the increase of which, either by working or by suffering, is alone to be cared for. What you give, give freely and without price, that others may prosper and have increase from you and your goodness. Thus you will be a truly good man and a Christian. For what to you are your goods and your works, which are done over and above for the subjection of the body, since you have abundance for yourself through your faith, in which God has given you all things?

We give this rule: the good things which we have from God ought to flow from one to another and become common to all, so that every one of us may, as it were, put on his neighbor, and so behave towards him as if he were himself in his place. They flowed and do flow from Christ to us; He put us on, and acted for us as if He Himself were what we are. From us they flow to those who have need of them; so that my faith and righteousness ought to be laid down before God as a covering and intercession for the sins of my neighbor, which I am to take on myself, and so labor and endure servitude in them, as if they were my own; for thus has Christ done for us. This is true love and the genuine truth of Christian life. But only there is it true and genuine where there is true and genuine faith. Hence the Apostle attributes to charity this quality: that she seeketh not her own.

We conclude therefore that a Christian man does not live in himself, but in Christ and in his neighbor, or else is no Christian: in Christ by faith; in his neighbor by love. By faith he is carried upwards above himself to God, and by love he sinks back below himself to his neighbor, still always-abiding in God and His love, as Christ says, "Verily I say unto you, Hereafter ye shall see heaven open, and the angels of God ascending and descending upon the Son of man." (John 1:51)

Thus much concerning liberty, which, as you see, is a true and spiritual liberty, making our hearts free from all sins, laws, and commandments, as Paul says, "The law is not made for a righteous man" (1 Timothy 1:9), and one which surpasses all other external liberties, as far as heaven is above earth. May Christ make us to understand and preserve this liberty. Amen.

Finally, for the sake of those to whom nothing can be stated so well but that they misunderstand and distort it, we must add a word, in case they can understand even that. There are very many persons who, when they hear of this liberty of faith, straightway turn it into an occasion of licence. They think that everything is now lawful for them, and do not choose to show themselves free men and Christians in any other way than by their contempt and reprehension of ceremonies, of traditions, of human laws; as if they were Christians merely because they refuse to fast on stated days, or eat flesh when others fast, or omit the customary prayers; scoffing at the precepts of men, but utterly passing over all the rest that belongs to the Christian religion. On the other hand, they are most pertinaciously resisted by those who strive after salvation solely by their observance of and reverence for ceremonies, as if they would be saved merely because they fast on stated days, or abstain from flesh, or make formal prayers;

talking loudly of the precepts of the Church and of the Fathers, and not caring a straw about those things which belong to our genuine faith. Both these parties are plainly culpable, in that, while they neglect matters which are of weight and necessary for salvation, they contend noisily about such as are without weight and not necessary.

How much more rightly does the Apostle Paul teach us to walk in the middle path, condemning either extreme and saying, "Let not him that eateth despise him that eateth not; and let not him which eateth not judge him that eateth!" (Romans 14:3)! You see here how the Apostle blames those who, not from religious feeling, but in mere contempt, neglect and rail at ceremonial observances, and teaches them not to despise, since this "knowledge puffeth up." Again, he teaches the pertinacious upholders of these things not to judge their opponents. For neither party observes towards the other that charity which edifieth. In this matter we must listen to Scripture, which teaches us to turn aside neither to the right hand nor to the left, but to follow those right precepts of the Lord which rejoice the heart. For just as a man is not righteous merely because he serves and is devoted to works and ceremonial rites, so neither will he be accounted righteous merely because he neglects and despises them.

It is not from works that we are set free by the faith of Christ, but from the belief in works, that is from foolishly presuming to seek justification through works. Faith redeems our consciences, makes them upright, and preserves them, since by it we recognize the truth that justification does not depend on our works, although good works neither can nor ought to be absent, just as we cannot exist without food and drink and all the functions of this mortal body. Still it is not on them that our justification is based, but on faith; and yet they ought not on that account to be despised or neglected. Thus in this world we are compelled by the needs of this bodily life; but we are not hereby justified. "My kingdom is not hence, nor of this world," says Christ; but He does not say, "My kingdom is not here, nor in this world." Paul, too, says, "Though we walk in the flesh, we do not war after the flesh" (2 Corinthians 10:3), and "The life which I now live in the flesh I live by the faith of the Son of God." (Galatians 2:20) Thus our doings, life, and being, in works and ceremonies, are done from the necessities of this life, and with the motive of governing our bodies; but yet we are not justified by these things, but by the faith of the Son of God.

The Christian must therefore walk in the middle path, and set these two classes of men before his eyes. He may meet with hardened and obstinate ceremonialists, who, like deaf adders, refuse to listen to the truth of liberty, and cry up, enjoin, and urge on us their ceremonies, as if they could justify us without faith. Such were the Jews of old, who would not understand, that they might act well. These men we must resist, do just the contrary to what they do, and be bold to give them offence, lest by this impious notion of theirs they should deceive many along with themselves. Before the eyes of these men it is expedient to eat flesh, to break fasts, and to do in behalf of the liberty of faith things which they hold to be the greatest sins. We must say of them, "Let them alone; they be blind leaders of the blind." (Matthew 15:14) In this way Paul also would not have Titus circumcised, though these men urged it; and Christ defended the Apostles, who had plucked ears of corn on the Sabbath day; and many like instances.

Or else we may meet with simple-minded and ignorant persons, weak in the faith, as the Apostle calls them, who are as yet unable to apprehend that liberty of faith, even if willing to do so. These we must spare, lest they should be offended. We must bear with their infirmity, till they shall be more fully instructed. For since these men do not act thus from hardened malice, but only from weakness of faith, therefore, in order to avoid giving them offence, we must keep fasts and do other things which they consider necessary. This is required of us by charity, which injures no one, but serves all men. It is not the fault of these persons that they are weak, but that of their pastors, who by the snares and weapons of their own traditions have brought them into bondage and wounded their souls when they ought to have been set free and healed by the teaching of faith and liberty. Thus the Apostle says, "If meat make my brother to offend, I will eat no flesh while the world standeth" (1 Corinthians 8:13); and again, "I know, and am persuaded by the Lord Jesus, that there is nothing unclean of itself; but to him that esteemeth anything to be unclean, to him it is unclean. It is evil for that man who eateth with offense." (Romans 14:14, 20)

Thus, though we ought boldly to resist those teachers of tradition, and though the laws of the pontiffs, by which they make aggressions on the people of God, deserve sharp reproof, yet we must spare the timid crowd, who are held captive by the laws of those impious tyrants, till they are set free. Fight vigorously against the wolves, but on behalf of the sheep, not against the sheep. And this you may do by inveighing against the laws and lawgivers, and yet at the same time observing these laws with the weak, lest they be offended, until they shall themselves recognize the tyranny, and understand their own liberty. If you wish to use your liberty, do it secretly, as Paul says, "Hast thou faith? have it to thyself before God" (Romans 14:22). But take care not to use it in the presence of the weak. On the other hand, in the presence of tyrants and obstinate opposers, use your liberty in their despite, and with the utmost pertinacity, that they too may understand that they are tyrants, and their laws useless for justification, nay that they had no right to establish such laws.

Since then we cannot live in this world without ceremonies and works, since the hot and inexperienced period of youth has need of being restrained and protected by such bonds, and since every one is bound to keep under his own body by attention to these things, therefore the minister of Christ must be prudent and faithful in so ruling and teaching the people of Christ, in all these matters, that no root of bitterness may spring up among them, and so many be defiled, as Paul warned the Hebrews; that is, that they may not lose the faith, and begin to be defiled by a belief in works as the means of justification. This is a thing which easily happens, and defiles very many, unless faith be constantly inculcated along with works. It is impossible to avoid this evil, when faith is passed over in silence, and only the ordinances of men are taught, as has been done hitherto by the pestilent, impious, and soul-destroying traditions of our pontiffs and opinions of our theologians. An infinite number of souls have been drawn down to hell by these snares, so that you may recognize the work of antichrist.

In brief, as poverty is imperiled amid riches, honesty amid business, humility amid honors, abstinence amid feasting, purity amid pleasures, so is justification by faith imperiled among ceremonies. Solomon says, "Can a man take fire in his bosom, and his clothes not be burned?" (Proverbs 6:27) And yet as we must live among riches, business, honors, pleasures, feastings, so must we among ceremonies, that is among perils. Just as infant boys have the greatest need of being cherished in the bosoms and by the care of girls, that they may not die, and yet, when they are grown, there is peril to their salvation in living among girls, so inexperienced and fervid young men require to be kept in and restrained by the barriers of ceremonies, even were they of iron, lest their weak minds should rush headlong into vice. And yet it would be death to them to persevere in believing that they can be justified by these things. They must rather be taught that they have been thus imprisoned, not with the purpose of their being justified or gaining merit in this way, but in order that they might avoid wrong-doing, and be more easily instructed in that righteousness which is by faith, a thing which the headlong character of youth would not bear unless it were put under restraint.

Hence in the Christian life ceremonies are to be no otherwise looked upon than as builders and workmen look upon those preparations for building or working which are not made with any view of being permanent or anything in themselves, but only because without them there could be no building and no work. When the structure is completed, they are laid aside. Here you see that we do not contemn these preparations, but set the highest value on them; a belief in them we do contemn, because no one thinks that they constitute a real and permanent structure. If any one were so manifestly out of his senses as to have no other object in life but that of setting up these preparations with all possible expense, diligence, and perseverance, while he never thought of the structure itself, but pleased himself and made his boast of these useless preparations and props, should we not all pity his madness and think that, at the cost thus thrown away, some great building might have been raised?

Thus, too, we do not contemn works and ceremonies—nay, we set the highest value on them; but we contemn the belief in works, which no one should consider to constitute true righteousness, as do those hypocrites who employ and throw away their whole life in the pursuit of works, and yet never attain to that for the sake of which the works are done. As the Apostle says, they are "ever learning and never able to come to the knowledge of the truth." (2 Timothy 3:7) They appear to wish to build, they make preparations, and yet they never do build; and thus they continue in a show of godliness, but never attain to its power.

Meanwhile they please themselves with this zealous pursuit, and even dare to judge all others, whom they do not see adorned with such a glittering display of works; while, if they had been imbued with faith, they might have done great things for their own and others' salvation, at the same cost which they now waste in abuse of the gifts of God. But since human nature and natural reason, as they call it, are naturally superstitious, and quick to believe that justification can be attained by any laws or works proposed to them, and since nature is also exercised and confirmed in the same view by the practice of all earthly lawgivers, she can never of her own power free herself from this bondage to works, and come to a recognition of the liberty of faith.

We have therefore need to pray that God will lead us and make us taught of God, that is, ready to learn from God; and will Himself, as He has promised, write His law in our hearts; otherwise there is no hope for us. For unless He himself teach us inwardly this wisdom hidden in a mystery, nature cannot but condemn it and judge it to be heretical. She takes offence at it, and it seems folly to her, just as we see that it happened of old in the case of the prophets and Apostles, and just as blind and impious pontiffs, with their flatterers, do now in my case and that of those who are like me, upon whom, together with ourselves, may God at length have mercy, and lift up the light of His countenance upon them, that we may know His way upon earth and His saving health among all nations, who is blessed for evermore. Amen.

In the year of the Lord
1520

The 95 Theses

1. Our Lord and Master Jesus Christ, when He said Poenitentiam agite, willed that the whole life of believers should be repentance.
2. This word cannot be understood to mean sacramental penance, i.e., confession and satisfaction, which is administered by the priests.
3. Yet it means not inward repentance only; nay, there is no inward repentance which does not outwardly work divers mortifications of the flesh.
4. The penalty [of sin], therefore, continues so long as hatred of self continues; for this is the true inward repentance, and continues until our entrance into the kingdom of heaven.
5. The pope does not intend to remit, and cannot remit any penalties other than those which he has imposed either by his own authority or by that of the Canons.
6. The pope cannot remit any guilt, except by declaring that it has been remitted by God and by assenting to God's remission; though, to be sure, he may grant remission in cases reserved to his judgment. If his right to grant remission in such cases were

despised, the guilt would remain entirely unforgiven.

7. God remits guilt to no one whom He does not, at the same time, humble in all things and bring into subjection to His vicar, the priest.

8. The penitential canons are imposed only on the living, and, according to them, nothing should be imposed on the dying.

9. Therefore the Holy Spirit in the pope is kind to us, because in his decrees he always makes exception of the article of death and of necessity.

10. Ignorant and wicked are the doings of those priests who, in the case of the dying, reserve canonical penances for purgatory.

11. This changing of the canonical penalty to the penalty of purgatory is quite evidently one of the tares that were sown while the bishops slept.

12. In former times the canonical penalties were imposed not after, but before absolution, as tests of true contrition.

13. The dying are freed by death from all penalties; they are already dead to canonical rules, and have a right to be released from them.

14. The imperfect health [of soul], that is to say, the imperfect love, of the dying brings with it, of necessity, great fear; and the smaller the love, the greater is the fear.

15. This fear and horror is sufficient of itself alone (to say nothing of other things) to constitute the penalty of purgatory, since it is very near to the horror of despair.

16. Hell, purgatory, and heaven seem to differ as do despair, almost-despair, and the assurance of safety.

17. With souls in purgatory it seems necessary that horror should grow less and love increase.

18. It seems unproved, either by reason or Scripture, that they are outside the state of merit, that is to say, of increasing love.

19. Again, it seems unproved that they, or at least that all of them, are certain or assured of their own blessedness, though we may be quite certain of it.

20. Therefore by "full remission of all penalties" the pope means not actually "of all," but only of those imposed by himself.

21. Therefore those preachers of indulgences are in error, who say that by the pope's indulgences a man is freed from every penalty, and saved;

22. Whereas he remits to souls in purgatory no penalty which, according to the canons, they would have had to pay in this life.

23. If it is at all possible to grant to anyone the remission of all penalties whatsoever, it is certain that this remission can be granted only to the most perfect, that is, to the very fewest.

24. It must needs be, therefore, that the greater part of the people are deceived by that indiscriminate and high-sounding promise of release from penalty.

25. The power which the pope has, in a general way, over purgatory, is just like the power which any bishop or curate has, in a special way, within his own diocese or parish.

26. The pope does well when he grants remission to souls [in purgatory], not by the power of the keys (which he does not possess), but by way of intercession.

27. They preach man who say that so soon as the penny jingles into the money-box, the soul flies out [of purgatory].

28. It is certain that when the penny jingles into the money-box, gain and avarice can be increased, but the result of the intercession of the Church is in the power of God alone.

29. Who knows whether all the souls in purgatory wish to be bought out of it, as in the legend of Sts. Severinus and Paschal.

30. No one is sure that his own contrition is sincere; much less that he has attained full remission.

31. Rare as is the man that is truly penitent, so rare is also the man who truly buys indulgences, i.e., such men are most rare.

32. They will be condemned eternally, together with their teachers, who believe themselves sure of their salvation because they have letters of pardon.

33. Men must be on their guard against those who say that the pope's pardons are that inestimable gift of God by which man is reconciled to Him;

34. For these "graces of pardon" concern only the penalties of sacramental satisfaction, and these are appointed by man.

35. They preach no Christian doctrine who teach that contrition is not necessary in those who intend to buy souls out of purgatory or to buy confessionalia.

36. Every truly repentant Christian has a right to full remission of penalty and guilt, even without letters of pardon.

37. Every true Christian, whether living or dead, has part in all the blessings of Christ and the Church; and this is granted him by God, even without letters of pardon.

38. Nevertheless, the remission and participation [in the blessings of the Church] which are granted by the pope are in no way to be despised, for they are, as I have said, the declaration of divine remission.

39. It is most difficult, even for the very keenest theologians, at one and the same time to commend to the people the abundance of pardons and the need of true contrition.

40. True contrition seeks and loves penalties, but liberal pardons
    only relax penalties and cause them to be hated, or at least,
    furnish an occasion for hating them.
41. Apostolic pardons are to be preached with caution, lest the
    people may falsely think them preferable to other good works of
    love.
42. Christians are to be taught that the pope does not intend the
    buying of pardons to be compared in any way to works of
    mercy.
43. Christians are to be taught that he who gives to the poor or
    lends to the needy does a better work than buying pardons;
44. Because love grows by works of love, and man becomes better;
    but by pardons man does not grow better, only more free from
    penalty.
45. Christians are to be taught that he who sees a man in need, and
    passes him by, and gives [his money] for pardons, purchases not
    the indulgences of the pope, but the indignation of God.
46. Christians are to be taught that unless they have more than they
    need, they are bound to keep back what is necessary for their
    own families, and by no means to squander it on pardons.
47. Christians are to be taught that the buying of pardons is a
    matter of free will, and not of commandment.
48. Christians are to be taught that the pope, in granting pardons,
    needs, and therefore desires, their devout prayer for him more
    than the money they bring.
49. Christians are to be taught that the pope's pardons are useful, if
    they do not put their trust in them; but altogether harmful, if
    through them they lose their fear of God.
50. Christians are to be taught that if the pope knew the exactions

of the pardon-preachers, he would rather that St. Peter's church should go to ashes, than that it should be built up with the skin, flesh and bones of his sheep.

51. Christians are to be taught that it would be the pope's wish, as it is his duty, to give of his own money to very many of those from whom certain hawkers of pardons cajole money, even though the church of St. Peter might have to be sold.

52. The assurance of salvation by letters of pardon is vain, even though the commissary, nay, even though the pope himself, were to stake his soul upon it.

53. They are enemies of Christ and of the pope, who bid the Word of God be altogether silent in some churches, in order that pardons may be preached in others.

54. Injury is done the Word of God when, in the same sermon, an equal or a longer time is spent on pardons than on this Word.

55. It must be the intention of the pope that if pardons, which are a very small thing, are celebrated with one bell, with single processions and ceremonies, then the Gospel, which is the very greatest thing, should be preached with a hundred bells, a hundred processions, a hundred ceremonies.

56. The "treasures of the Church," out of which the pope grants indulgences, are not sufficiently named or known among the people of Christ.

57. That they are not temporal treasures is certainly evident, for many of the vendors do not pour out such treasures so easily, but only gather them.

58. Nor are they the merits of Christ and the saints, for even without the pope, these always work grace for the inner man, and the cross, death, and hell for the outward man.

59. St. Lawrence said that the treasures of the Church were the Church's poor, but he spoke according to the usage of the word in his own time.

60. Without rashness we say that the keys of the Church, given by Christ's merit, are that treasure;

61. For it is clear that for the remission of penalties and of reserved cases, the power of the pope is of itself sufficient.

62. The true treasure of the Church is the Most Holy Gospel of the glory and the grace of God.

63. But this treasure is naturally most odious, for it makes the first to be last.

64. On the other hand, the treasure of indulgences is naturally most acceptable, for it makes the last to be first.

65. Therefore the treasures of the Gospel are nets with which they formerly were wont to fish for men of riches.

66. The treasures of the indulgences are nets with which they now fish for the riches of men.

67. The indulgences which the preachers cry as the "greatest graces" are known to be truly such, in so far as they promote gain.

68. Yet they are in truth the very smallest graces compared with the grace of God and the piety of the Cross.

69. Bishops and curates are bound to admit the commissaries of apostolic pardons, with all reverence.

70. But still more are they bound to strain all their eyes and attend with all their ears, lest these men preach their own dreams instead of the commission of the pope.

71. He who speaks against the truth of apostolic pardons, let him be anathema and accursed!

72. But he who guards against the lust and license of the pardon-

preachers, let him be blessed!

73. The pope justly thunders against those who, by any art, contrive the injury of the traffic in pardons.

74. But much more does he intend to thunder against those who use the pretext of pardons to contrive the injury of holy love and truth.

75. To think the papal pardons so great that they could absolve a man even if he had committed an impossible sin and violated the Mother of God–this is madness.

76. We say, on the contrary, that the papal pardons are not able to remove the very least of venial sins, so far as its guilt is concerned.

77. It is said that even St. Peter, if he were now Pope, could not bestow greater graces; this is blasphemy against St. Peter and against the pope.

78. We say, on the contrary, that even the present pope, and any pope at all, has greater graces at his disposal; to wit, the Gospel, powers, gifts of healing, etc., as it is written in I Corinthians 12.

79. To say that the cross, emblazoned with the papal arms, which is set up by the preachers of indulgences, is of equal worth with the Cross of Christ, is blasphemy.

80. The bishops, curates and theologians who allow such talk to be spread among the people, will have an account to render.

81. This unbridled preaching of pardons makes it no easy matter, even for learned men, to rescue the reverence due to the pope from slander, or even from the shrewd questionings of the laity.

82. To wit:–"Why does not the pope empty purgatory, for the sake of holy love and of the dire need of the souls that are there, if he redeems an infinite number of souls for the sake of miserable

money with which to build a Church? The former reasons would be most just; the latter is most trivial."

83. Again:—"Why are mortuary and anniversary masses for the dead continued, and why does he not return or permit the withdrawal of the endowments founded on their behalf, since it is wrong to pray for the redeemed?"

84. Again:—"What is this new piety of God and the pope, that for money they allow a man who is impious and their enemy to buy out of purgatory the pious soul of a friend of God, and do not rather, because of that pious and beloved soul's own need, free it for pure love's sake?"

85. Again:—"Why are the penitential canons long since in actual fact and through disuse abrogated and dead, now satisfied by the granting of indulgences, as though they were still alive and in force?"

86. Again:—"Why does not the pope, whose wealth is today greater than the riches of the richest, build just this one church of St. Peter with his own money, rather than with the money of poor believers?"

87. Again:—"What is it that the pope remits, and what participation does he grant to those who, by perfect contrition, have a right to full remission and participation?"

88. Again:—"What greater blessing could come to the Church than if the pope were to do a hundred times a day what he now does once, and bestow on every believer these remissions and participations?"

89. "Since the pope, by his pardons, seeks the salvation of souls rather than money, why does he suspend the indulgences and pardons granted heretofore, since these have equal efficacy?"

90. To repress these arguments and scruples of the laity by force alone, and not to resolve them by giving reasons, is to expose the Church and the pope to the ridicule of their enemies, and to make Christians unhappy.

91. If, therefore, pardons were preached according to the spirit and mind of the pope, all these doubts would be readily resolved; nay, they would not exist.

92. Away, then, with all those prophets who say to the people of Christ, "Peace, peace," and there is no peace!

93. Blessed be all those prophets who say to the people of Christ, "Cross, cross," and there is no cross!

94. Christians are to be exhorted that they be diligent in following Christ, their Head, through penalties, deaths, and hell;

95. And thus be confident of entering into heaven rather through many tribulations, than through the assurance of peace.

Appendix I: About Martin Luther

Martin Luther was born in 1483 in Eiselben, Saxony—a town located in what is now modern-day Germany. His father, who was of peasant lineage, started out as a miner but worked hard to improve his family's situation. In time, Hans Luther became a well-to-do businessman who owned several mines. Seeing promise in his young son and knowing from experience the difficulties of mining, Hans had high hopes that young Martin would be a lawyer and not a miner.

Hans could afford to send Martin to school, and he did. After completing studies in Magdeburg and Eiselben, Martin enrolled in the University of Erfurt. There he earned the degree his father desired him to—the one which put him well on the path to becoming a lawyer.

Everything changed for young Martin, however, in July of 1505. His life-changing moment came during a terrifying thunderstorm. In the midst of lightning flashes and thunder crashes, Martin cried out for help to St. Anne, patron saint of the miners.

"Save me, St. Anne, and I'll become a monk!" he shouted above the thunder. The storm quickly subsided and Martin—much to the consternation and grief of his father—set out to fulfil his vow.

The life of a medieval monk, which was anything but easy, required enormous physical and mental sacrifice. The Augustinian monks, or friars as they were called, slept little, prayed eight times a day, and performed painful penances—among other distasteful tasks. Immersed in a culture of self-mortification, the monks engaged in rituals designed to demonstrate their humility, faith, and endurance as a way of purging their sins. Fasting, manual labor, begging for food, sleeping on hard benches without blankets or even out in the snow were all disciplines which monks frequently undertook.

The life of a monk, which was hard anyway, was made harder by Martin's dreadful fear of hell and the wrath of God. In his search for peace and salvation, Martin engaged in the self-mortifying austerities of monkhood with zeal and devotion. Despite his herculean efforts, however, Martin did not find the peace or spiritual enlightenment he craved so badly. Plagued by a sense of inner spiritual emptiness, he chastised himself continually for his failings and sinful nature.

When Martin shared his struggles with a superior, he was given more work to keep his mind off the subject. Another mentor advised Martin that, by focusing his life exclusively on Jesus, he would be provided with the guidance he so badly wanted. This was more helpful to Martin. After continuing his religious studies as an Augustinian friar, Martin was ordained in 1507. Little did he know that in a few short years his thinking would once again be altered—in a way that would change the world.

Martin's second life-changing experience came about in 1510, when, at the age of 27, he was sent to Rome as a delegate to a

Catholic church conference. Appalled by the immorality and corruption he witnessed in Rome, Martin returned to Germany discouraged and disillusioned. In an attempt to suppress his spiritual turmoil, he enrolled in the University of Wittenberg to further study religion. There he excelled in his studies, earned a doctorate, and became a professor of theology.

During this time Martin spent more and more time studying Scripture—and it was his study of the Scripture, rather than his advanced education, that finally opened his spiritual eyes. While preparing a lecture on the epistle of Romans, Martin stumbled across the powerful words of Romans 1:17 "the just shall live by faith." Fascinated with the meaning of the verse, Martin ruminated on it for quite some time. Suddenly, everything became clear in a way that would transform not only Martin's life, but much of the Christian world. Martin now understood that the key to salvation wasn't self-mortification, demonstrations of piety, or religious dogma. It was faith alone—in the atoning blood of Jesus Christ—that would bring salvation! This realization brought about a marked change in Martin's life. It also planted the seed that would set the Protestant Reformation in motion.

In those days, the Roman church commonly sold "indulgences," which were promises of forgiveness for sin and freedom from punishment. By paying large sums of money, church members could purchase redemptive relief for either themselves or their deceased relatives who, without their financial intervention, might be writhing in purgatory.

As Martin continued to study the Bible, he saw clearly that the practice of selling and buying indulgences was wrong. When Pope Leo X mounted a fundraising campaign to build St. Peter's Basilica in

Rome, with the goal of raising money through the sale of indulgences, Martin decided the time for action had come. Johann Tetzel, one of Rome's most successful fundraisers, was making the rounds with a large treasury chest. Tetzel is credited with the little fundraising slogan

"The moment a coin in the coffer rings,

A soul from purgatory springs!"

The people, who weren't anxious to have their relatives in purgatory—or visit that dread destination themselves for that matter—gave generously. Instead of giving, however, Martin Luther got busy with his pen. In October of 1517, he sat down and wrote the "95 Theses," a devastating, Bible-based critique of the sale—and purchase—of indulgences as a corruption of faith.

Little did Martin know, when he nailed a copy of the "95 Theses" to the University of Wittenberg's chapel door, that they would serve as much more than the discussion triggers that he had envisioned. Aided by the newly invented printing press, copies of the "95 Theses" spread to receptive ears throughout Germany within two weeks of his posting. Within two months, Martin's "propositions" had been circulated throughout Europe.

In addition to the sale of indulgences, Martin called some of the basic tenets of the Roman church into question. He believed and taught that:

- The Bible, rather than church doctrines, fathers, or traditions, should be the guide of faith,
- The pope was not infallible, and
- Christians are saved through faith in Jesus, rather than through their own efforts or monetary payments to the church.

Martin followed his "95 Theses" with a series of pamphlets explaining his views.

Within a year of the posting of the "95 Theses," the Catholic church began trying to stop the spread of Martin's ideas. In October 1518, Cardinal Thomas Cajetan, by authority of the pope, ordered Martin to recant his "95 Theses." In response, Martin stated that he would not recant unless Scripture proved him wrong. He also continued to lecture and write in Wittenberg, just as he always had.

Things came to a head in 1519 when Martin publicly denied that the pope was the only one who could properly interpret the Bible. That statement, which was considered to be a direct attack on the authority of the pope, was not well-received in Rome. Soon Martin received an ultimatum from the pope threatening him with excommunication if he didn't change his views. The ultimatum, which came in the form of a letter, was publicly burned by Martin on December 10, 1520. The very next month, Martin was officially excommunicated from the Roman Catholic Church.

After excommunicating Martin, Pope Leo X summoned the reformer to appear at an assembly known as the "Diet of Worms." Martin did appear before the assembly, where he was once again urged to recant. Martin refused, stating that: "unless I am convinced by the testimony of the Scriptures or by clear reason (for I do not trust either in the pope or in councils alone, since it is well known that they have often erred and contradicted themselves), I am bound by the Scriptures I have quoted and my conscience is captive to the Word of God. I cannot and will not recant anything, since it is neither safe nor right to go against conscience. May God help me. Amen."

In response, the Catholic church banned Martin's writings and declared him to be both a heretic and an outlaw. Under the protection of some German princes, Martin made his escape and went into hiding in Wartburg Castle.

Martin's seclusion turned out to be a blessing, for it gave him time to translate the New Testament into the German language. As a result of his work, ordinary people were able to read God's word. This in turn radically changed the relationship between church leaders and parishioners, as the people could, for the first time, read and interpret the Bible for themselves.

While at Wartburg Castle, Martin was contacted by a group of nuns who wished to escape the rigors of convent life. The reform-minded nuns somehow slipped a letter to Martin pleading for help.

With the help of a fish salesman, Martin orchestrated a daring plot. The nuns were smuggled out of the convent after dark, hidden in a wagonload of herring barrels. The escape, though punishable by death if foiled, was documented by one local student, who wrote that "a wagon load of vestal virgins has just come to town, all more eager for marriage than for life. God grant them husbands lest worse befall."

Martin tried to get the women's families to accept them back, but they refused—possibly because of the civil penalties involved. Over the next two years, he managed to find homes or husbands for all except the strong-willed Katharina von Bora, who refused all suitors except Martin himself. Martin wasn't sure if he should be married, but after a time he relented and took Katharina as his wife.

Though still under threat of arrest, Martin left Warburg Castle and moved back to Wittenberg with Katharina. From Wittenberg, with the help of some German princes, Martin and his followers organized the Lutheran Church.

Despite the somewhat scandalous marriage of an ex-monk to an ex-nun, the couple—and their marriage—prospered. Katharina was a great help to Martin in his ministry, and in time, the couple had six children. A shrewd businesswoman, Katharine greatly increased the couple's wealth by investing in farms, orchards and even a brewery. She also converted a former monastery into a dormitory and meeting center for Reformation activists. In the years to come, Martin wrote some humorous things about his marriage experience. In a nod to the strong-minded nature of his wife, he affectionately referred to her as "Lord Katie." And in another reference to his marriage, he mentioned that by marrying Katie, he had "made the angels laugh and the devils weep."

During the years 1524-1526, a number of peasants (the leaders of which used Martin's arguments to justify their rebellion) revolted. Despite his own peasant roots, Martin denounced the uprising and sided with the rulers. Martin lost many supporters because of this stance, but the Lutheran Church continued to grow. His anti-Semitic views, as exhibited in some of his writings later in life, also placed him in the path of controversy—at least in modern times.

From 1533 to his death in 1546, Martin served as the dean of theology at University of Wittenberg. During this time his health deteriorated and he suffered from several illnesses, including arthritis, heart problems and digestive challenges. Martin Luther passed to his rest on February 18, 1546 following a stroke, at the age of 62 years old. He was buried in Wittenberg, the city he helped turn into an intellectual center.

After his death, Martin Luther's teachings and Bible translation continued to radically change Christianity. Thanks in large part to the invention of the Gutenberg press, the Protestant Reformation that

Martin Luther sparked continued to grow in popularity and strength. Today, this great German theologian is considered to be one of the most influential figures in the history of Christianity.

Printed in Great Britain
by Amazon

Unfortunately, many people think the Christian walk is loaded with so many rules and regulations that Christians are virtually slaves to an ever-demanding God. This is in contrast to the truth of the Scriptures, which clearly teach that God—rather than burdening His children—desires to set them free. The freedom God offers is the central thesis of "On Christian Liberty," where Martin Luther teaches that true freedom is found only through submission to Christ.

Luther declares his purpose for the book when he writes, "To make the way smoother for the unlearned—for only them do I serve—I shall set down the following two propositions concerning the freedom and the bondage of the spirit: A Christian is a perfectly free lord of all, subject to none. A Christian is a perfectly dutiful servant of all, subject to all."

Bolstered by many Scripture references, this relatively short book has no chapters but proceeds along a logical train of thought. Liberty in a Christian sense is described as our faith which simultaneously compels us forward to live fruitful, productive lives while liberating us from the law, works, or other burdens that hinder us. As Luther wrote, "Yes, since faith alone suffices for salvation, I need nothing except faith exercising the power and dominion of its own liberty. Lo, this is the inestimable power and liberty of Christians."

ISBN 9798645984533

90000

9 798645 984533